feelers, flippers and feathery bits

look book

The Tweenies love animals.
They like learning about
how animals live, what they
eat and how they move.

Fizz loves fish. Max is showing her a video about creatures that live in the sea near Australia.

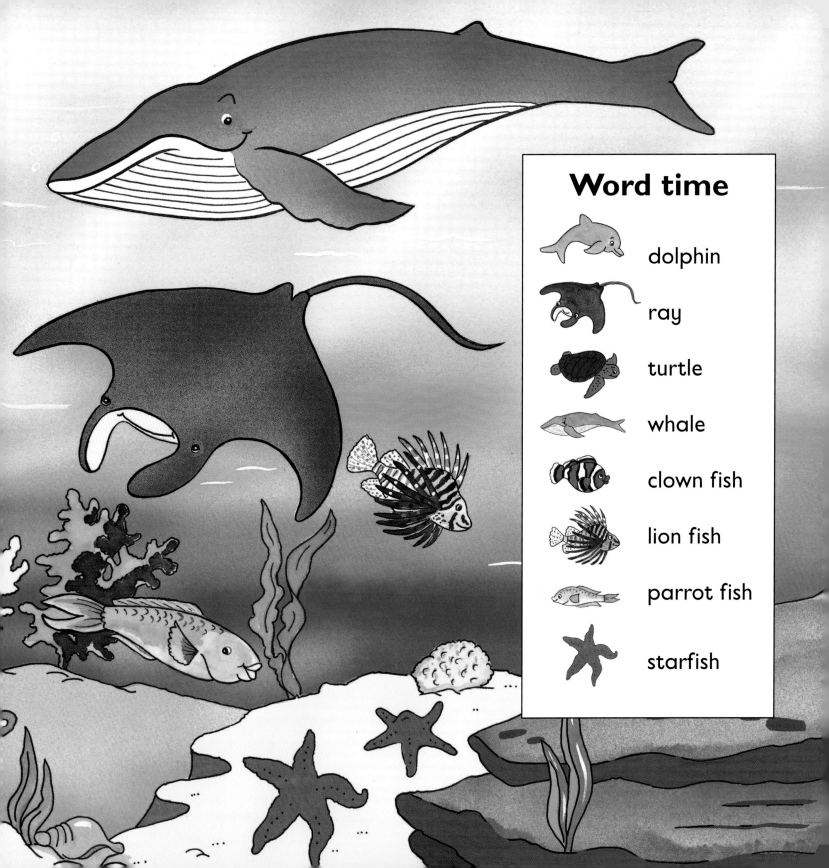

Word time

dolphin

ray

turtle

whale

clown fish

lion fish

parrot fish

starfish

Max takes Fizz to the
aquarium. An aquarium is
a special place where lots
of fish and other water
creatures live. Max asks the
fish keeper to show Fizz the
sea horses – they're her
favourite animal.

fish from the Atlantic Ocean

sea horses

salmon

skate

octopus

shark

dogfish

eel

shell

lobster

crab

starfish

telly time

Jake loves animals. Judy is showing him a video about lots of wild African animals.

Word time

cheetah

ostrich

warthog

gazelle

lion

wildebeast

giraffe

Judy takes Jake to a city farm to look at the different animals that live there. He likes to watch them as they eat and play.

leaping goat

crawling tortoise

pecking hen

trotting pony

waddling goose

jumping rabbit

messy time

Make your own aquarium

When Fizz gets back to the playgroup, she shows Jake how to make an aquarium picture. Use the patterns to make your own aquarium wall.

You will need:-

apron

 card

round-ended scissors

glue

different coloured sheets of paper

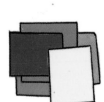

1) Trace one of the patterns on to card and cut it out with round-ended scissors.

2) Decorate your creature with different coloured bits of torn or cut paper. Glue the small pieces of paper on to your animal.

3) When your fish or sea horse is dry, display it on your wall.

Bella loves anything that flies. Max shows her a video about the flying animals of South America. They live in a tropical rainforest.

Word time

toucan

humming bird

macaw

flamingo

vulture

butterfly

Max takes Bella to a butterfly house, where they look at beautiful butterflies. Bella learns how a caterpillar turns into a butterfly.

1) The adult butterfly lays eggs.

2) The eggs begin to grow and then hatch open.

3) A tiny caterpillar comes out of the egg.

4) The caterpillar eats leaves.

5) The caterpillar spins silk around itself. The silk turns into a hard case called a 'pupa'.

6) After a few days, the pupa breaks open and a beautiful butterfly comes out.

telly time

Milo loves jungle beasts. Judy is showing him a video about animals that live in the jungles of Africa.

Word time

chimpanzee

lizard

leopard

bullfrog

snake

butterfly

Judy takes Milo to a safari park where animals can live in big open spaces. Judy and Milo drive around the park in a special truck with the animal keeper.

cow

male chimp

female chimp

young chimp

family of chimpanzees

family of elephants

bull

calf

family of zebra

stallion

mare

foal

lioness

lion

cub

family of lions

Make your own mask

When Milo gets back to playgroup, he wants to make a mask.

You will need:-

apron

 card

round-ended scissors

lump of modelling clay

pencil

paints and brushes

strips of crêpe paper

1) Trace the monkey face on to a piece of card and cut it out.

2) Ask a grown-up to cut out the two eye holes for you.

3) Ask a grown-up to punch out one hole on either side of the mask, near the ears, using a pencil and a lump of modelling clay.

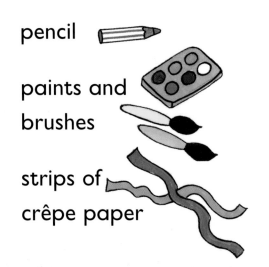

4) Paint your chimpanzee mask.

5) When it is dry, thread some strips of crêpe paper through the holes and tie your mask around your head.

The Tweenies have had a wonderful time learning about feelers, flippers and feathery bits. They have made fish and sea horses to decorate their rooms, and great masks to wear. What a busy time!